# Wide Open

David Hill

illustrated by Jennifer Cooper

Leon's best friend, Bart, was always telling
him to close his mouth. But every time
Leon really concentrated on something,
his mouth just opened.

At the swim meet, Leon's mouth opened
as he crouched on the edge of the pool,
waiting to dive in. When he did dive,
he swallowed nearly half the pool!

During the class debate, Leon was thinking
so hard about what to say that he stood
up with his mouth open, and an insect
flew in. "Ladies and gent– Yurrk! Aarrk!"
he spluttered.

Leon and Bart worked together on their project for the Technology Fair. "We're making paper airplanes," Bart told Mrs. Ponti.

Their teacher frowned. "Paper airplanes?" As Leon thought about how to explain, he felt his mouth hanging open. He shut it so quickly that his teeth clicked.

Bart explained instead. "We're going to show how different-shaped airplanes fly in different ways."

"OK," said Mrs. Ponti, "but be careful where you fly those things!"

Leon practiced every night at home. He folded airplanes so that they flew straight, turned sideways, or dived down. Without telling Bart, he practiced making a special airplane to throw last of all.

The morning of the fair came. The school hall was packed with kids and displays. There were robots and experiments and huge colored graphs. "Our display's so ordinary," Bart muttered.

Then it was their turn to present their project. Leon and Bart threw airplanes that flew perfectly straight, airplanes that turned left or right, and airplanes that dived down or swooped up. Things went OK, but Leon knew that it didn't look all that special.

Then came the last airplane, the one Leon had practiced and practiced with. It was designed to swoop up, turn left, and then land perfectly at his feet. He'd folded it carefully and bent its wings so that it would do everything it was supposed to.

But Leon couldn't be sure. When he'd practiced, the airplane had swooped up OK, but the left turn and perfect landing had only worked sometimes. Would it work today?

The hall was silent. Everybody was watching Leon. He lifted the airplane. He found that his mouth was open, so he closed it. He threw.

Leon had aimed slightly down so that the airplane would swoop up. "Up!" he called silently to it. "Go up!"

It did. "Yeah!" cheered the watching kids. Leon's mind sent more orders to his airplane. "Turn left!" he told it. "Turn left!"

It did – a perfect left turn. "Wow!"
breathed the kids. Leon was concentrating
as hard as he could as he kept sending
orders to the airplane. "Glide down!
Come on! Glide down!"

It didn't. Instead, the airplane made
another perfect left turn and flew straight
on … straight into Leon's open mouth!
Leon shut his mouth – fast. His lips
closed around folded paper. The airplane's
front half was inside his mouth. The back
half stuck out.

For a moment, there was total silence.
Then yells and cheers burst out.
"Wow!" "Awesome!" "Cool!"

With half the airplane still sticking
out of his mouth, Leon bowed to the
audience. More cheers and clapping
burst out. He sneaked a look at Bart.

Bart was standing, completely amazed,
with his eyes popping out and his
mouth wide open.